EACH IN A PLACE APART

Phoenix Poets

A SERIES EDITED BY ROBERT VON HALLBERG

JAMES McMICHAEL

Each in a Place Apart

THE UNIVERSITY OF CHICAGO PRESS
Chicago and London

James McMichael is the author of three previous books of poetry, *Against the Falling Evil, The Lover's Familiar,* and *Four Good Things,* as well as of a study of James Joyce entitled *"Ulysses" and Justice.* He is professor of English at the University of California, Irvine.

The University of Chicago Press, Chicago 60637
The University of Chicago Press, Ltd., London
© 1994 by The University of Chicago
All rights reserved. Published 1994
Printed in the United States of America
03 02 01 00 99 98 97 96 95 94   1 2 3 4 5

ISBN: 0-226-56106-2   (cloth)
       0-226-56107-0   (paper)

Library of Congress Cataloging-in-Publication Data

McMichael, James, 1939–
    Each in a place apart / James McMichael.
        p.   cm. — (Phoenix poets)
    I. Title.   II. Series.
    PS356.A31894E24   1994
    813'.54—dc20   93-31265
                                            CIP

EACH IN A PLACE APART

At school, I was a
squad-leader. I'd gotten enough votes. It meant
I'd wear as bandolier over my white T-shirt
a red cotton sash. It meant I'd say who'd play left field.
She was back in the hospital. My father saw her
every day. Though she was usually about the same,
tonight she was better. He took me to the
Crown Cafeteria, my favorite place to eat.
Waiting for the light so we could cross Colorado,
he said she'd died. The stairs to his office echoed.
Through the front windows we looked out over the street.
I was sitting in his lap in the big swivel chair.
  "But you said she was better."
  "She *is* better. This is better."

The small, pretty woman at the station.
Where would she sit? Eager, tanned and brash, a soldier
followed her to the wide rear seat, I followed too but
stopped, tried not to listen, I was fourteen. Incredibly,
she moved. Could she sit with me? She was on her way
home from her sister's, she'd been there while her husband
closed things up in Fresno, where they'd lived before.
Did I like Utah? She did and didn't, and why.
My answers to her reasons spared me the tight
stultifying fear that I would touch her, her hand was
there but I wouldn't touch it, I could breathe, I managed
even to turn toward her when she talked. We went on to
families, mine first, her questions intimate and long.
She never betrayed it if she thought me young
but she wasn't flirting. I wasn't confused, I knew
right where I was with her: I was lost. It was getting
dark outside and we were hungry. We bought sandwiches in
St. George. Back on the bus, she said she hadn't
slept well the night before, I said she should put her
head on my shoulder if she wanted to. A quick pleased
hum in her throat as she skewed toward me, nestled,
and complied. Past Las Vegas, where she woke a little,
lifted it and then let it rest, her head
stayed on my shoulder. She slept. That was what mattered.
My vigil was to know that I could leave and not disturb her.
She held me just above the elbow with her left hand.
Wanting more and more to thank her and to say goodbye, I
knew she'd sleep beyond my stop and wake and think about me
mostly that I must have left.

My parents had teased that if I ever
caught a fish I'd take it to bed. Warm lakes had
catfish. Trout were the fish I wanted. They were in the
mountains that abided out of view in almost every
Western I saw. In the benign ephemeral first frames with
boardwalks and tethered horses, frontages, a cloudless day,
kill was promised. More alluring were the extras.
They were harried sober people. The women had
children with them sometimes, and of the men,
any one might even then be on his way to rent a
pack train at the stables. This man had started planting
fingerlings in the high lakes six years before. They'd taken.
Having seen good brood stock there, he was heading
back to them now with his mules and tins and would
parcel them out. Until Mike Cady got his car
(he'd be buying it in June and then we'd go),
the *Inyo-Mono Fishing News* had pictures of big
rainbows and browns. They couldn't have been the last.
Above the canyons in the valleys that rose lake by lake,
there were others with the same pearl underbellies,
the same intransigent ways. Some shorelines dropping
headlong toward them through the top clear zones,
it was easy for me to translate into any equal
volume of water the air inside the tall green
handball court walls. Each was somewhere in a given cube.
The water touched their noses, it touched their sides. Hungry,
beautiful and secret, they held to the beryl half-light,
the sunken boulders opaline and faint. Mike and I had brought
sheepherders' bread and a can of black olives.
No one had been in there yet ahead of us over the snow.
Near the top, where the lake was, Mike said he was sick.
He got in his sleeping bag and didn't want to talk.

There was sun left only on the Inconsolables
and they were orange with it and riven, glacier-backed.
I fished a little in the outlet, which had thawed.
How deep the drifts would be at every saddle in the long
profile of the crest. Basins on the other side were
three days from any trailhead. Missing my dad,
I knew I should eat something, I knew I'd be awake all night.

A highway runs the
length of the peninsula. The suburbs overlap.
She lived in one of them and took around with her
her setting. Shops and houses, luminous spring lawns,
streets that led off to places she'd speak French.
Unpunctured by the phrase "One evening" or "One fine day,"
her setting promised it would yield the longed-for.
We met one evening at church, but the adjacent
backyards, the balm of their untold repository
waiting in the dark as, introduced, we
looked at one another, looked away. 1964,
November, but the earth, its different settings for
still other stories, its planes of lines extending and
reversible at any point. Saltflats. An abandoned
tinker's van in a swampy field. The wooded island
upstream from the bridge, the one down.

Nor was it even then too late. I was the
married, reliable sponsor to her youth group,
I had to keep it to myself. Away from her, inside me,
it would suffocate, I thought, if I stayed busy.
My body kept it alive. What if she weren't
there again for a third straight week? I should
want her not to be there. Love meant wanting her to be
comely, prized and occupied, light-spirited, it meant
wanting her not to want me. Another Sunday and she
wasn't there. If I told her, would she want me then?
I couldn't tell her, couldn't not, and did.

I wanted for her sake to undo it,
I asked her to forget. There wouldn't be
time for us since I was married. I'd made her want
another time, when, whole, impossibly together,
we'd rescue my avowal, which was a curse.

Though I asked her not to, she went on
waiting for that time and, by the tree where I
couldn't get away to meet her, waiting
undismayed, heartsick, eighteen.

When she ushers at an outdoor evening concert,
I meet her at the side gate. She can stay until ten.
On a bicycle to the eucalyptus grove, she brings her
This England book. She'd been there with the
parents of a friend one summer and wants to show me
London and the Cotswolds, Chester, Blenheim, Rye.
Standing on a felled tree, she pulls my head to her shirt.
Every time for us is a rehearsal for September 8th
when we'll say good-bye. We know we'll write. We write
daily for a year. By thinking that on her way
south sometime to see her grandmother I'd have
two hours with her in Union Station, I hold on.
My walk toward her from the car, her seeing me, her
face and how she'd feel against my chest. Of those
last minutes with her there would be a first, then others
after it, their series welling at my wrists and temples.
She'd let go of me, she'd turn to get her train and we'd have
lived it, we'd remember, it would have to be enough.
She writes that she is changing schools. Should she be
four hundred miles away or only sixty?

Surprised at my surprise that I can say
"Sid Kitrell's house . . . , Tim Shirley's . . . ,"
she's next to me in the car, I'm showing her where
I'd lived, Lucile's, my father's office, with her
next to me she leads me to connect for her as many
disregarded things as I can say, I say them,
make them her things too and Pasadena
street by street is comfort, it's Linda and comfort,
the afternoon awash with her sure care.

It wouldn't be fair to us for her to lie.
Whole days with me have made her days alone much harder.
I'm not to worry. She just needs to get her
strength back. It helps that she can see me in a month.
She thinks she's sharing me, thinks I'm not
all hers. I can't tell her otherwise and
stay married. We write and phone, I keep seeing her.
There's no good way out.

In my stupid arithmetic, we're
outnumbered, she and I, by my wife and two sons.
Barbara doesn't notice any change. We visit her
parents. Her dad and I go fishing. Bobby's in school.
Linda never asks me to leave them, never says she'll
leave me. We promise only that we'll meet next
week again at Vicki's or at Chuck's. The quick
assurances each time, we're fine, it's again been
less than too hard and here we are. Then always
rapture and protestation, doubt, self-doubt, and
lingering, the future that we're sure we've lost
forever there for us in our clothes on the cold floor.

Back with her family the second summer,
she guides foreigners around the campus,
learns from the escort to an Argentine the little
training she would need to do his job.
Letters are her way to show us both that she can
stay busy, nothing in what she does too small to tell.
How she's doing she gauges by where it doesn't
hurt her to go. To be somewhere we'd been and not be
hurt by it is to love me well, to be glad it's
me she loves and not someone she could both
love and be with. Because she'd looked for me there
one Sunday when I didn't come, the quad is hard.
So's the amphitheater, the benches under the oaks.
After breakfast once, she walks to Lagunita.
At the far shore, children with balloons run on
ahead of their parents. The water is still.
She sits for a long time on an old railroad tie.
Everything about the morning is quiet and bright.

At eleven she'd been mother to her mother's twins,
was Queen of the May at twelve. Her parents drank.
She wasn't to go to bed without saying
goodnight to her mother. Every night her mother
told her she was bad. Her mother was right. She was
bad not to love her mother, which her mother knew.
Her mother also knew that she loved other people.
Did she love them so that she could hurt her mother?
It hurt no one for her to love places.
Her favorite story was about a place two children
went to meet a third. It was a walled place with
tall trees. The door to it was overgrown because
they weren't supposed to go there, no one was to go
inside, that world so gray with disaffection
it looked dead. They tended to the plants and borders,
listened always for some grown-up who might find them out.
Someone was there. As she came toward them she smiled.
The third child said
     "It's mother—that's who it is!"
and then again
     "It's mother!"

"A picture that scares me has gone through my mind
several times in the last few weeks. I see myself
sitting in front of a fire and being very lonely,
needing you very much. I have a husband and children
and feel very unfulfilled. You aren't near enough so I can
see you and Margie is far away, in fact the house is
out in the middle of hundreds of leafless trees,
the leaves are on the ground. It's absurd in some ways
because I could never live that far away from
other people. I can't imagine children who wouldn't
keep me from being lonely. The husband is a dolt.
I wouldn't marry a dolt but I must not have found
anything as good as you and me again and that scares me."

She hates loving to be with me, I with her.
I have angina, cancer of the testicles.
Staggered against my pulse to their own odd beat,
spasms in my left eardrum last three or four
days at a time. As they slacken, I count how many
breaths I can steal before the next one pops.
She lets me tap them out on the back of her hand.
I can't get them right. My finger is late.
I have to keep saying
    "No, not then"
and, still alone with them, start over, thinking we're
both crazy, how can it matter and could she maybe
hear them with her ear against my ear?

She writes that yesterday had been very good.
Carol wanted to talk and so they went to the beach.
The ocean was a wonderful, stormy color.
She knows it would have to be a quick look but would I
do something for her? Would I come see her room on
Friday at nine? We won't be seen. She promises.
Everyone would be gone then and I could cross the
church parking lot to her back door. That's where she is now.
The orchids are next to her on the bench in the sun.
A jay is covering something up with leaves.
I have ten minutes of class left, she writes, and am
probably not thinking about her. She wants to know what
page I'm on in the book we're both reading.

Everything is in the way. If it's just
Barbara and the boys who stop us, I see them
anywhere, in common bodies, there are calculable
miles of them between our house and Linda, between it and
Linda in five years. She and I will be
through then and I'll go on seeing, I'll think
daily not to drive somewhere we'd been. Even as I
wait for her here and know that maybe in the next
look behind me I will see her car, it's still
Holmby Park, triangular, genteel, its huge trees
hiding what would show in section if they were
split from the top and didn't fall, if they were split
again and didn't and again until they weren't
dark anymore inside. The darkness is their store of
times they've been seen as backdrop to a face seen
one last time. It won't be today we'll add to it.
We'll walk a little and then go to Vicki's,
we'll come back later for the other car.

I know I'll lose her.
One of us will decide. Linda will say she can't
do this anymore or I'll say I can't. Confused
only about how long to stay, we'll meet and close it up.
She won't let me hold her. I won't care that my
eyes still work, that I can lift myself past staring.
Nothing from her will reach me after that.
I'll drive back to them, their low white T-shaped house
mine too if I can make them take her place.
I'll have to. I mustn't think her room and whether if by
nine one morning in a year she will have left it,
sleepy, late, remembering tomorrow is New York,
her interview with UN General Services a
cinch to go well. What I must think instead is Bobby's
follow-through from the left side. He pulls my lob past Geoff,
who's bored. Shagging five soaked balls isn't
Geoff's idea. I tell him he can hit soon. He takes his time,
then underhands the first off line and halfway back.
Ground fog, right field, the freeway, LAX. She has
both official languages. For the International Court,
"The Registrar shall arrange to have interpreted
from French to English and from English into French
each statement, question and response." Or maybe it will be
Washington she'll work for. On mission to a new
West African republic, she might sign on with
Reynolds, Kaiser, Bethlehem Steel. They needed Guinea's
bauxite for aluminum, manganese from Gabon,

their dealings for more plants and harbors slowed by lengthy
phonecalls through Paris. When there were snags, she'd
fly there that same afternoon, her calendar a mix of
eighty hours on and whole weeks off. There'd be
sidetrips to England by Calais and one aisle
over from her on the crossing, by himself,
the man I saw this week I fear she'd like.
He'd have noticed her before they cleared the dock, she'd been
writing something, left wrist bent toward him, the card almost
filled, now, with whatever she'd been telling someone else.
She'd start another, the address first. Eased that he'd
sense it in his shoulders when she stood to leave,
he'd keep himself from looking, it was much better
not to look, he might not interest her, better
not to be left remembering how she looked.
Dover. He'd follow her to the train and sit
across from her, apply himself convincingly to his four
appointments and their dossiers. After she'd make
notes to herself from a bed and breakfast guide,
from *The Guide to the National Trust,* she'd put the books
back in her hemp bag. He didn't mean to be
nosy, he'd say, but was she going to
see some country houses while she's here? Comfortably,
she'd tell him which ones. Though he knew them all, he'd be so
taken with her that he'd lose what she was saying,
he'd undergo the list and ask if she'd be
hiring a car. She'd pick one up tomorrow in
Hammersmith and then drive west. Would she have
dinner with him tonight? She'd say she'd like that:
she was booked at the St. Margaret's, off Russell Square,
could he meet her there at seven? When she'd close her eyes,
her head against the cushioned wing of the seat,
he'd think her managing to rest was not so much a
carelessness to his attentions as that she wasn't vain.

She wouldn't catch him watching if he angled his look away from her toward the window, in the tunnels especially he'd see reflected in its glass her gradual ˙ full outline as she breathed. There would be time all evening to talk. He'd tell her then about his uncle's place in Surrey where they'd both be welcome, its rubble-stone and leaded casements, tile, an east loggia to the lawns and wooded slope. He'd loved the kitchen garden as a boy, the path there, silver lavender and catmint borders, an oak-doored archway framing for him on chains above a well the twin coronas of roses in the cool damp light.

Nothing is more delicious or remote: after
dinner some night in our own place, I bring her tea.
I can't tell her that. Telling it would say these
meetings of ours are far too little, it would hurry us
beyond them to the time we give them up. And there is
Easter. Over the long weekend, my wife takes the boys
away with her to see friends. We have four days,
more than we'd ever hoped for or think we'll have again.
We don't know what to do with them. Why can't we
save them for later when we aren't this close to having
just what we want? Locked in their icy cirques,
the lakes in the Sierra are three months away,
we can't go there. Or if we did go, what if the car failed,
what if we had to leave it to be fixed? Though safe is
my way, not hers, she doesn't argue. We have
sand-dabs in San Clemente. We drive to Oceanside.
Back at Chuck's, I'm afraid to turn on the lights.
Friday is all right but it seems best that she go
home to the Y. I go home. A few days later
I tell her on the phone I'm leaving them.

To get away from the house to see her
I'd kept pleading work. The library at school was
quieter, I'd said, the kids weren't there. It had served,
though they weren't troublesome or loud. Now, I sit them
next to one another, tell them I'll be moving
away for awhile, that I'm going to live
somewhere else. Nothing from Geoff, from Bobby
instantly a chuckle and smile.
    "Are you happy? Why did you laugh?"
    "Because now we won't bother you when you have to write."

My wife is taking it well enough.
If there's another woman she doesn't want to know.
In LA, where no one knows us and would tell,
I rent a studio above a garage. Linda moves
out of the Y to the front unit of a duplex.
She's at the Ambassador for Bobby Kennedy's
victory party the night I leave. Dumbfoundedness,
one more impossible cortege, but she can come
over now, I can go see her, summer, our walks up the
fireroad in the last light, rabbits and even
deer sometimes across the reservoir on the grassy fans.
We go to the store together. There's time for
movies, now, and double solitaire. We wrestle.
She cuts my hair one Saturday outside her kitchen.

I have to teach again that fall and move back
down to Laguna. The days alone are less baleful,
they're just for a year. No one ever stops by,
but when she drives down on Thursdays after class
I meet her at the Tic-Toc Market. My apartment's
little more than the bed, and we can't wait.
Safe-harbored, whispering, with always more to tell,
we stay put, the dark catching up with us each week
until it's there in our first hour. From upstairs,
the muffled after-dinner clatter. Somebody's phone.
We start over at her knee, we're slower, the prolonged
fine sadnesses we'd hoarded from the years before
slow to give way and slowing so that only after
nothing for awhile does what we're doing take us
not toward her finishing again (or not right now) but
anywhere we've missed, her ribs, only the lightest
grazing of them, down and forward, not too far
nor too far back again across, each furrow
closer by its width to that last ridge below the pliant
dominating compass of her breast. We're being
pulled, of course. She hasn't stopped me. She won't.
At its outermost, her body's what she touches with.
It isn't long before she's moving too. Our skins
poised for the next just barely altered place, we're
thread-like stalks, light-running, sheer, our tiny leaves
flush with the basin's wide paved curb. It's still
gate-piered courtyard, ashlar dressed, a balustrade.
From jets above the circular pool alcoves,
water, its affection for an always lower point
tight-channeled in the iris rills, then underground,
the land dropping away through poplars to the dell.
Damp peaty banks easing to the full pond-hollow,
I'd never married, she'd been born to someone else.

Souls. Unconsulted, wet, they're given
breath to, they breathe, there's no time out, they can't work
trades for another's chances, can't sort through their own from
afterwards to write them as they'd have them be.
In the book of all-knowing, the parenthesis
before one's year of birth is there as shield against
the years amassed outside it. It would have taken less than
one of them to have broken through, a moment only,
change with his first moment or with hers that moment you
yourself broke through the cervix and you're either,
this cartoonist walking past you to his car
or a bonneted and aproned wayside gossip slumped
forward on the low stone wall. She isn't wanted
back at the house for hours and hears firsthand what the
kitchenmaid had told her Rose had seen. They were mostly
clothed, Rose said, and on their knees, atremble, Miss Letty
bracing herself in front on both shoulders.
The wood was its long hilltop strip, their quarter of it
dark, unfrequented. Rose had passed absently
across the lane, not down along it and around.
Quiet enough to let her see them first,
she'd pretended she'd seen nothing and was on her way
she couldn't say where. Disheartened, nervous, cold,
they'd recomposed themselves, said what they could to comfort,
taken their separate ways back. Rose, a talker,
knew something now that doomed them. They would be watched.
It had been hard enough already not to hate
their differences in station. Willfully, for months,
Letty had seen him each late afternoon when he carried
back from their daytime storage off the hall
the library's electric lamps. Then last week she'd
timed it wrong, had caught him in his green and yellow livery

groping about under the big table with the plugs.
He wasn't angry, she could tell, because he'd had to
keep himself from smiling. But she'd learned they didn't
fit here anymore. Since their dizzying
unthinkable espousal, the only places common to them
had been places they'd hid. Withy Copse was safest
but it left less time. Nearer, there were stands of hazel, ash,
the thicket halfway to the upper farm. Now that
Rose knew, the intervals afforded them by trees were
closed, they couldn't reach them unseen. Their mischance was
thickness. They had parts that blocked the light.
Knowing each other's schedule to the quarter hour,
each guessed where the other was and stayed away.
As what seemed to them at first no more than caution
stretched into weeks, their smuggled letters feigned
new dispositions of the heart that neither of them
credited or would deny. He wrote that it had
hurt him for a while to know he wouldn't touch her
ever again, but that was over: this way was simply
best for him. And for her too, she answered,
looking for a glimpse of him across the lawn.
In their counterfeit accord, the letters stopped.
Had she stopped wanting him? He couldn't tell.
From overlays of being seen that, never touching, hovered
just at the skin, they'd now pulled back through
veins and tissues to their deep recallings.
His brooding often passed its twin from her midway.
Their jealousies were interdictions. Neither dared
ask about the other. Both feigned wanting to hear.
So well kept was their secret now that each was left
unsure that there was anything to hide. Whatever
rumors there were had not cost him his position.
He took another. Letty stayed. Between them,
indeterminate and nothing-wanting, numinous, that

angel they'd made, the child she'd never carry.
Nothing had happened that last interrupted time. He'd
heard Rose, turned and seen her go. Because he'd only
started to be through just then but wasn't through,
the egg had not been visited by sperm. Earlier,
it had divided from its flooded lymphoid sac,
the threads around its spindle pairing off, dividing,
ready for division once again if through secreted
mucus and the one canal one swimmer
made its way there. Instead, the world was full.
Though Letty had made room for him, there wasn't room for
microfilaments and microtubules, foci, any
orderly partitioning that meant the cells would do
one thing or other but not all. So that instead of
changes that foretold a break within it, there was still
the same bright plenum as before, the interbedded
limestones and clays, escarpment, camber, dip, an
east-draining valley, its assemblages of quarried stone,
its souls. Within the one intelligence of how they'd fare,
the landed and their tenantry were one. What hadn't
changed for them, what couldn't, was the one light of all
possible lucks and bodies. There was the one filled light.
Engendering, diffuse, it went on drawing out
along with itself to their utmost sides all things that
enter into composition. However tardy, we were
latent there ourselves, Linda and I. The one time it's thrown,
each of us has his and her own fatally-obtained number.
The lot that falls to any couple might have been ours.
To the history of marriage and divorce, we hadn't been
born yet, our births were forestalled. Class wouldn't do us in.
Neither would faith. We'd be subject to only the most
genial of prohibitions. Though I couldn't join her on
her side of our separate pasts, we weren't to be
lost to the world as lovers are who in their longing

die or go mad in patience and alone. Which
shirt she'd wear, our pounds-to-dollars ledger, her lost stamp—
light's traverse of all surfaces would show these too.
We'd face a butcher's window once we'd parked.
The high street would be almost empty.
Since from the millrace and the bridge we'd set out
left across it for a tussocky far slope,
that parish was our quitclaim, it had already
ministered to us from its reserves. For as many
hours as all its parts are by themselves,
setting is the chance that something good might happen.
It's entire for that time, no person's there to see as
different and overt the single gateposts, single
free- and leasehold fields. The park wall, its fallen coping
thatched over in a growth of nettles. A twig-bearer's
strong straight flight. Some tofts. Five rushlit cottages.
The places on the ground between the trees.

Except when there's fog,
we can see from our long front window the huge
supertankers and the half-day boats. There are California
gray whales in the winter. I'm through writing by
lunchtime usually if I've gotten a good start,
and on afternoons I'm not at school, there's
reading to do. When I'm at my best with it,
its phrases are as much in league as I want
things for us to be. When I follow to the letter first
this phrase, this one, and now this and this,
they feel looked back on from a time so ample
that whatever has been hoped for is made whole. I'm not
married now. Linda's not alone. I'd gotten almost
used to it the other way. Before, the five or so
hours a week we'd managed for ourselves meant
all the rest were double. Wherever I was, I'd
double it by thinking Linda, it was those places
she was that I should be too. She'd made there be
more for me than what was at hand. I'd come to
need more. There'd never be time, never anything
ahead of us but more hiding. I needed scenes in which
place itself was perfectly the only thing that took place.
Though "the lake would not be so good a painter
if it did not first paint me," I wasn't there to turn
the obviousness of any hill or rock inside.
Air had allowed a range of bodies to crowd it out.
Of those the wind played with, few were irritable.

All could enlarge the earth's surface by as much as themselves. Lines that might otherwise have shown led in from maritime and inland floors. Each river was at once everywhere in its watershed. With their boughs and sprays touching and interlaced, looms of vegetation reached continuingly into their own pasts for more shade still. No two movements were the same, nor no two leaves. Measure was kept waiting. "What ails thee?" didn't have to be asked.

She'd loved it when at fourteen she'd gone to school in
Switzerland. Her mother wasn't there to read her mind.
In curlers and quilted robes, the girls had smuggled
leftovers up the back stairs. They'd gotten to go skiing.
She could see Evian across the lake after a good rain.
Though she'd had to go home when the year was over,
she was learning French. It had let her feel she could be
good at something, that her mother was wrong. While she'd
waited to be loved and wasn't, there'd been at least
French for her, as it would be there for her later while she
waited for me. Now that she's finished her
degree in French, she wants to be in diplomatic service.
We're on the wrong coast. She starts translating Sand's
Histoire de ma vie. She takes a part-time library job
and finds the work's all right.

Our house is a winter rental. Each June, we
store everything we don't take with us in the camper to
Idaho and Montana. It's two full days' drive with
desert much of the way, then farms. Only in the
last half hour, past Ashton, up the hill, are there
logging roads and lodgepole, spruce and fir.
It agrees with us to be outdoors all summer.
I'm shameless about how much I want to fish the broad
wadeable meadow streams. The new mayflies can't
lift themselves from the surface film until their
wings dry. When I watch them drift down over the slack water,
disturbances are rocks sometimes and sometimes fish.
Linda does needlepoint and crossword puzzles. She keeps
checklists of the flowers she finds on her long woodland walks.
We do our wash in town and play cards in the hotel lobby.
We have time to read. By August, there are berries.
A six-pack of Grain Belt beer is ninety-nine cents.
Friends have a ranch with acres that stretch back through
bottomland to their mountain pasture. The old
Hodges' place is vacant. They ask us to stay.
In the upstairs bedroom under the cottonwood,
it's almost dark when it clouds up late in the afternoon.
We find cancelled checks in the homestead down by the creek.
Lots are for sale. In our fifth summer there, we buy one.
A contractor frames a house for us which I have
six weeks to enclose. I want to be, but I'm not
good at it, it doesn't please me at all when my rip-cut
splinters the cedar batten, I miss the stud
completely with a second nail and I throw things and scream.
She can't stand it when I'm like this. But though she has to
leave sometimes and not come back for hours, the work gets done.
We drain the pipes, hang shutters, close the place up.

She wants more time to herself once we're back home.
So she can be alone there from noon on, I stay away.
It's harder to work. My journal entries circle.
Unless I stop writing them about our chances,
we don't have a chance. It seemed much better
last week than this. Am I too upset to tell?
I ought to keep myself from making resolutions.
She'll have to see I'm on my own to want me back.
For her, it's day to day. Now that she's doing
graduate work, she has people to speak French with.
Some of them are men. There's probably one she looks
forward to seeing, as she doesn't me, and why
should she, my explosions are her mother's, my having made her
wait those years was what she was used to from the two of them.
In my not leaving Barbara and the boys to be with her,
Linda could again be hopeful, I was being her
parents again, who'd maybe this time give. That was our luck.
Alternate Fridays had sustained us in it, we'd been
together in thrall to the occasional late
Sunday afternoon. She's given all that up as hapless.
Being mated, having me as her mate: it comes to
nothing for her, nothing would be hers to move
away from if she moves from me. Though I
might have left them sooner if she'd asked,
I'm the reminder that she didn't. I tell myself I'll
meet someone else, that I'm companionable after all.
On the weekends, if she's staying home, I drive
up into the hills. Though I'm not any
abler than I was last month to let her go,
I'm practicing. For minutes at a time, a book
holds me away from her and I'm alone.
Her classes keep her busy. We go on bumping

into one another in the kitchen, we share the car.
It isn't until Christmas that she thinks we're all right.
She asks me to come with her to a party.
We're talking more. There are our nightly
little deaths again, and our trips to Westwood.
We watch *The World at War* and *Upstairs, Downstairs,* golf.
Bobby and Geoff are with us every third weekend.
We make a treasure hunt for them in the lot next door.

She gets her M.A. Since she's still working
part-time only in the library, we have
whole summers in the mountains. She plants an alpine
rock garden with a wall and pond. But like going again to
Europe, where we'll stay for a year, whatever she does proves
daily to her that she's waiting. If she'd gotten a good
job by now, or if she'd sold a book, it would be as much
her schedule we were on as it would mine. It's not that way.
A man in Michigan will do an essay she's translated
if she gets the rights. He should have asked for them
himself, the publisher in Paris tells her: she isn't a
millionaire, is she, that she can pay for them on her own.
I want there to be the respite for her of where we are,
am nervous about it too. Without her French and Italian,
I'd be lost. The skylight in our flat is a hatch that opens.
Standing on a chair, my head above the level of the roof,
I see the whole north slope of our deep transverse valley.
We buy duty-free a radio that picks up Munich.
When they go out alone by shortwave into the first
overture to _Leonore,_ the violins are
major, tentative, their slow five rising notes a clear fine
pencil of rays over the Tyrol and the high cols.
There are caves below the ridge where Partisans had
hidden from the Fascisti. In the summers only,
goatherds stay there now. So do trekkers caught in storms.
The peasants pay with sandals, sausages and wine
when they come down to see a doctor or for tools.
Disliked and well-to-do, a bachelor, the baker tends at
four each morning to the ovens and the tubs of dough,
then stands outside his shop all day in the blind street.
A black-bordered poster there tells that someone has died.
It's November. On a terraced plot a third of the way up,

bells from the other side are faint enough that what
wind there is must be from the lake. Crossing the
river again on our way back over the old bridge,
lights at the field are on already. I have to be
goalie in our pick-up soccer game or not play, I'm
bad with my feet. Though we have the place here until March,
she thinks that she'll go back to Paris, she'll canvas the trade:
there has to be something she hasn't found that she can try.
She doesn't want me to come with her. Having someone
caring how it goes would make it worse.

An editor in London tells her that he needs to have
translated from the French the third of a
six-volume history. A donor to the press had
murdered the second volume, the reviews had said.
Looking for someone new, they like Linda's sample from it
very much and want the rest by Christmas.
There's room in our flat for each of us to work.
We won't leave for months, but I'm already
missing every Pont Street Dutch facade. These were
her places first, she brought me to them, they were her best
prospects half her life ago, now they've delivered, she has a
book to do, she's happy, it's there to see, I want to
fasten inside me in its sum the way our mews looks,
want to learn by heart which buses take us where.
Twice through the outer boroughs the river bears
west a little, even. Islanded, embanked, it's still
tidal there, the wakes below its balks and pilings
hard to make out. Of the towns in sight of it upstream,
the smaller are set back the widths of churchyards.
It's tree-lined for a field or two on one side only.
From far enough above to show each turn,
reaches of it leave thumbs and bays in the flint gravel.
Tracts of barley and the bright coarse grasses fit
irregularly along it over the floodplain,
the mouths of its feeder-creeks hidden in green flags,
a single cream-white camas spearing
up through the ferns to the tip of its tall sheaf.
I've been restless for her for almost an hour when I
hear her come in. She'd had a good time swimming.
   "The sun was shining through the roof into the pool."

The original she's working with is
lazy and gnarled, there's at least as much
editing to do as there's translation. She has each
morning for it, and new purpose, notebooks, her Larousse.
Even when she stays at it into the afternoon,
we still have time for an outing, it's light until nine.
She reads to me on the drive that "the pond will be a
happy one for its lilies if it has near it
some wooded rising ground to shut it in,"
and from the summerhouse on stout oak posts we see
a clover meadow, fields, the chalk escarpment,
then pass the staging for the seed-trays on our way out.
Inside a row-house at the end of the small village,
the double sound of a door meeting its frame and latch.
Weekenders live here now, and a few widows. There's a rep for
industrial motors too, an estate agent, a diver whose
job it is to repair pipeline in the North Sea.
Through a gate she has to close, a young girl leads a pony.
Lorries sweep the grasses back on both sides of the deep lane.
The few last isolated showers have stopped. A man comes
out to brush the rain from his hydrangeas. We're home by dark.
After dinner, a short walk, the BBC, then going to sleep
next to her and waking, her being there to touch. Bobby's
Bob now. He flies over for our last few weeks, flies
back again when we fly to New York. Though we're in
transit for the summer, she averages her two
pages a day. We don't know it yet, but taken up with
work and friends and travel, we'd for the first time ever
forgotten where we were in the month. She's unaccountably
sanguine about the letter waiting for her at home.
It tells her that the donor has found out and won't
have it that he'd been passed over. The press is

sorry and embarrassed. It will of course by
all means pay her for her time.

After five years of saying it, it became a
joke with us that we'd have a baby in five years.
We're waiting for the EPT. Sitting as far
away from it as she can and still be home, she wants
me to be the one to read it. I'm surprised how
glad I am. Her not being glad lasts half an hour.
She'll work for the library until she's due in June.
The baby does its tours inside her. When we put the big
headphones on her tummy, it seems to hear.
Her doctor tells her to cut down on salt, her
blood pressure's high. We buy a stethoscope and cuff.
She tells Linda to quit her job and go to bed.
The salt-free cottage cheese is cardboard, but it's
not working, nothing is, I can wait until she's been
resting for an hour before I take it, it doesn't help.
Since her diastolic number's always high, it's of
course high when she sees the doctor: she'll be in the
hospital tomorrow morning if we don't change
doctors tonight. La Leche League has two it recommends.
The one who calls back asks everything. If she were
his wife, he says, he'd want her in the hospital.
We're too frightened to sleep. I hold her. I fall off
only when it's almost light and by then the
birds have started. It makes her cry to hear them.
When she's admitted to the ward, they hook an
IV up to her that hurts her hand. On the vacant bed
next to her, there's a tray with a syringe and drugs:
if she goes into labor she might have convulsions.
They tell us on Monday that the baby wouldn't be able to
breathe yet on its own, on Wednesday that it could
suffocate inside her, her placenta's shutting down.
They'll do another amniocentesis in the morning,

they'll take the baby in the afternoon. She and I are such
cases by now that I think they'll lie, they'll want to
quiet us for the birth by telling us the baby's lungs
are ready, that stranger things have happened in three days.
A nurse comes in and says the baby's lungs are ready,
let's go to prep. Since Linda can't have it
naturally, it matters all the more to her that she at
least be awake. She'll get to be. Both doctors
promised me this morning that she'll have a local,
it's up to them. I get scrubbed. Everyone's in greens.
Down a corridor, away from me so I won't hear,
the anesthesiologist is talking to her doctors,
who are very intent. The scene breaks up. Her doctors
don't have to tell me, I know already, I want to
hit them, I say I'd promised her because they'd promised,
I'd told her she could be awake, that I could
be there with her. Stop it, you can't let her
see you like this, her pediatrician says.
She's partly sedated. I tell her I'll be waiting
right down the hall. From another room than hers, a
baby, a first cry. I have to hear it or not listen too for
our baby, Linda's asleep, she can't. If it's from
her room now that I'm hearing something fainter,
someone should tell me soon. I believe the nurse who says
    "I can't tell you *what* it is, but it's really good."
    "How is Linda?"
    "They're sewing her up now, she'll be fine."
There's no reason not to believe her, Linda's
not going to die, she's not going to die or have to
hate it that she didn't, her baby's all right, we haven't
killed it by not changing doctors. It won't have to be
breathed for by a machine. Almost a month early, he's a
wonder to the staff at five pounds ten, he's Linda's doing,
she should be proud of him, she'll nurse him and she'll heal.

I can buy her now the blue- and white-checked gingham
mother and baby rabbit. I can buy her a robe. He comes
home with her after the weekend. The two of them feel so
hallowed to me that I'm slow to tell it hasn't worked
out for her at all. She writes an essay about it.
His having been taken from her early means she failed.
Bodies are bodies. They know things, they have their own ways.
She could have done it if she'd gotten the chance. Her doctor
didn't want Linda caring how things went. That had to be
her job, not Linda's. She'd gone on to say it almost
proudly of Linda at the last:
      "This little girl would be fine if she didn't have a brain."
It's a long essay. I recognize everything but me.
Not her antagonist, exactly, I'd been another
thing she'd had to worry. Whenever I'd taken her
blood pressure, she'd felt blamed by me if it was high.
Each crisis had been hers to deal with by herself.
Too busy or aloof to find her a better doctor,
I'd taught my classes, read, worked on my poem.

She's at the mirror.
I need to get behind it to the aspirin,
do so, close it.
"Goodness you wake up with a lot of headaches."
"Sorry."
"Don't be sorry, I'm sorry for you."
Surprised that it turned out like that, and
hating her, hating what I'd heard in my own voice,
I get out of her way. From the privacy of
brooding on it in another room, I hear what she meant:
"Congratulations. As good as you are at headaches,
why settle for so little, why not work up a
malignancy of some kind?" And I remember that
yesterday, when we were getting in the car, she winced.
She's always twisting her neck or back or something,
so I didn't ask her "Did you hurt yourself?" but
"Did you hurt yourself again?"

Impatience, most of all. She tells me that what
she wants when she's impatient with me is that I be
patient. Why am I so upset? Maybe because it's
time to be upset, how should I know,
    "I can't stand the way these fuckers drive their cars."
She tries not to watch me, has been seeing me
rave like this for twelve years and still isn't
used to it. I'm cooler now and look over at her.
Wanting to see at least the disguise of a smile,
I put my hand on her leg. She goes on looking
straight ahead at nothing, keeps it up for another
ten minutes. Domestic farce. Filler. Too little of the
exceptional in what we do from day to day as the
same two people. She knows me too well, each of us
knows too much about the other. Impatient for some
change in the other's nature that we think won't come,
we pout and blow up, dissemble, vex, forgive, go
on with it into the next instances of our
wishing we lived alone.

I want her sense of me to be wrong, want there to be
more than she sees, or something better, she reminds me
too much of what I can't do. The way she has of being
right about me is power. I can tell she thinks I'm distant.
I won't give in, I'll prove to both of us that I'm not.
Talking will distract her. I don't force it,
don't try to sound too cheery. But I'm telling her things I
wouldn't have—I'm saying them badly, distantly,
maybe even on purpose. She asks me
    "Is it me?"
    "No."
    "Then what?"
    "Nothing."
And I haven't lied, it's nothing, only power.

She likes to be out. Because he keeps us
in more, I help with the baby. She goes out
but wants me to go with her. Though I
go sometimes and like it, I'm sure that she's
insatiable, she's sure that I'm not liking it enough,
and it stays that way. The rest of the time is
mine, the time my writing takes becoming
proper to me, another of my properties, like my
cold hands. I remind her that my work's no fun.
She hadn't forgotten, she says, and neither am I.
It isn't a writer's line, but I say it.
    "You want me to be someone I'm not."
    "You want *me* to be someone I'm not and I'm
being that person."

As he often does when Linda holds him,
he pulls my fingers to his face. First it's a
nostril that he covers and uncovers languidly
again and again, then it's an eye. He keeps them moving.
If he could make my fingers fit him as her water did,
if my fingers were her water, it would always have been
his doing to have left it there, to have taken it away.
He's invented his Baby Kitties and the Six-year-olds.
Do they do that too? The question makes him sleepier.
As silly as they come, he smiles and goes on dabbing
closed and open, closed and open.

Three years not so much of squabbles as of
routine. Her days in the library, mine at
school and at home. Owen is four. We see friends for
dinner sometimes, talk on the phone to other friends
too far away. We go to Idaho in the summer.
I feel my life is safe because she loves me.
We'd been asleep, twelve years ago, when the
call came about my father. I went downstairs to
answer it, came back, her face asking me who
was it and I told her what. Then her
     "No,"
her arms held out to me from the sheet, her body,
the fathomless spare nurturing
     "O Jimmie"
which I still hear in anything she says.

One Saturday they go with friends to a police
bicycle auction. I stay home to write. By noon, the
Dodgers are on. I turn the sound off and read *Huck Finn,*
which I have to teach. When she comes in with groceries,
she's enraged at me. I'd stayed home to watch a game?
Defensive and chagrined, I can't get her to stop.
She hasn't been this mad for months. I don't cook or
garden with her. I don't dance. Couldn't I not work at least
one morning a week? The auction was fun. She'd kept thinking
how much I would have liked it.

She has to find a new job. It won't
do for her to stay at the library part-time. She's
liked there, the people like her. More and more, it's to
her they come when there are differences. She thinks they
listen to her. Maybe she'd be good in personnel.
She isn't saying it, but she regards as
failures of hers the things she's stayed with. The list goes
far enough back that if before it there'd been
something to draw from now, she doesn't feel it's there.
Having talked all evening, and later, here in bed,
we've been quiet for awhile before she says it.
    "I've got to do it right this time."
"Career" is what I should be hearing. More than anything
else has in our almost twenty years, it scares me
that she means me too.

It's early March. She doesn't know if we've
changed for her, but she's looking forward to June,
she wants me to go to Idaho without her. I'm afraid to.
She'll like it here too much without me and won't
want me to come home. It may already have been
weeks ago that I should have seen it, I can't stop watching,
will we make it or not? She doesn't know. Sometimes she's
hopeful that she'll get the spark back, the one I have for her.
Sometimes she thinks she wants another baby. I
can't let her see I'm cheered. Each time's a chance to
show her that her backs and forths don't matter.
If she feels monitored, it will drive her away.
Something in me touches her for a moment. When she
kisses me at Carl's Jr. while I'm standing in line,
I have to look at her. And if it's for
that moment only that she loves me, I can't hide.

This is more than just our worst fight ever.
She's wanting back the years she's given me, but I'm
right here with her and she can't decide.
It surprises her when I move to an apartment.
Evenings there are the hardest. Going to
sleep once, I don't inhale and wake myself up.
It's the ordinary things that give me the most trouble.
I can't read the sports section. For as long as I've been
opening my office door, she's been in my life.
Though I don't ask to, she says I can come home for
weekends, if I like. Everything seems so
effortless one morning that I tell her
    "You seem better."
    "For now, anyway."
We spend an hour pretending I hadn't slipped.

"You two are a great puzzlement to me,"
our therapist says as Linda hurries out
ahead of us down the hall, late to a meeting in her
new job. She thinks our years together have been her fault.
When I left Barbara and the boys to be with her,
I'd done so much she couldn't bring herself to hurt me.
She knows now that she should have told me no.

I move the rest of my clothes out of the house.
Our fights about money pass. In having to
leave her, I also have to think again the most
forgettable of our outings. Over the years, we'd taken our
bodies along in company to certain places. In
front of me a little, to the left, she'd answered "Yes" to
"Two for dinner?" I wasn't thinking, at the time, how I
fit into what she cared about: she fit for me. It comes
back to me now because I have to change it, I'd
gotten it wrong. Normal, expected, there's a brittle
politeness between us when I stop by to pick up Owen.
Below the hem of her flannel housedress, her bare feet.

The author would like to express his gratitude to the following publications, in which parts of *Each in a Place Apart* first appeared: *The Paris Review,* Fall 1988: "A highway runs the length of the peninsula," "Nor was it even then too late," "I wanted for her sake to undo it," "When she ushers at an outdoor evening concert," "In my stupid arithmetic," "Back with her family the second summer," "To get away from the house to see her." *The Missouri Review* IX, no. 3, 1986: "She's at the mirror," "Impatience, most of all," "I want her sense of me to be wrong," "She likes to be out," "Three years not so much of squabbles." *Agni* 29/30, 1990: "Surprised at my surprise," "It wouldn't be fair for us," "She hates loving to be with me," "'A picture that scares me . . . ,'" "She writes that yesterday had been very good," "Everything is in the way," "Nothing is more delicious or remote." *Verse* 5, no. 1, 1988: "The small, pretty woman at the station." *TriQuarterly* 83, Winter 1991/92, and *The Best American Poetry 1993*, ed. Louise Glück and series ed. David Lehman, New York: Colliers Books, 1993: "I know I'll lose her," "My wife is taking it well enough," "I have to teach again that fall." *American Poetry Review*, Jan.–Feb. 1994: "Except when there's fog."